CONTENTS

Words in the glossary appear in **bold** type the first time they are used in the text.

THE INVENTION OF BASKETBALL

Many sports have unclear beginnings, but not basketball! James Naismith invented basketball in 1891 in a school in Springfield, Massachusetts. Naismith, a teacher, wanted to create a new sport that **engaged** bored students. He combined pieces of different games. He wanted the ball to be thrown into a box but could only find peach baskets. He kept the bottom of the baskets connected.

The game was so enjoyed that it spread quickly. Certain stars and teams have made basketball one of the most popular sports in the world today.

Sports Stars, Stats, and Stories

BASKETBALL STARS, STATS, AND STORIES

BY BERT WILBERFORCE

INVESTIGATE!

Please visit our website, www.enslow.com. For a free color catalog of all our high-quality books, call toll free 1-800-398-2504 or fax 1-877-980-4454.

Library of Congress Cataloging-in-Publication Data
Names: Wilberforce, Bert, author.
Title: Basketball stars, stats, and stories / Bert Wilberforce.
Description: Buffalo, New York : Enslow Publishing, [2025] | Series: Sports stars, stats, and stories | Includes index. | Audience: Grades 2-3
Identifiers: LCCN 2024032717 (print) | LCCN 2024032718 (ebook) | ISBN 9781978542525 (library binding) | ISBN 9781978542518 (paperback) | ISBN 9781978542532 (ebook)
Subjects: LCSH: Basketball–Juvenile literature. | Basketball–Miscellanea–Juvenile literature. | Basketball players–Juvenile literature.
Classification: LCC GV885.1 .W537 2025 (print) | LCC GV885.1 (ebook) | DDC 796.323–dc23/eng/20240726
LC record available at https://lccn.loc.gov/2024032717
LC ebook record available at https://lccn.loc.gov/2024032718

Published in 2025 by
Enslow Publishing
2544 Clinton Street
Buffalo, NY 14224

Copyright © 2025 Enslow Publishing

First Edition

Designer: Andrea Davison-Bartolotta
Editor: Therese Shea

Photo credits: Cover, p. 1 (court) Prophotoo/Shutterstock.com; cover, p. 1 (hoop) Dan Thornberg/Shutterstock.com; cover, p. 1 (scoreboard) claudiuslower82/Shutterstock.com; cover (whistle) Billion Photos/Shutterstock.com; series art (banners) WinWin artlab/Shutterstock.com; series art (fact box background) EFKS/Shutterstock.com; series art (jersey texture) Kwangmoozaa/Shutterstock.com; series art (tablet) Lemberg Vector studio/Shutterstock.com; p. 4 FocusStocker/Shutterstock.com; pp. 5, 19 (main) Tullio Saba/Flickr.com; p. 6 File:Pete Maravich 1967.jpeg/Wikimedia Commons; pp. 7, 23 (right) John Mac/Flickr.com; pp. 8, 17, 25 (main) PCN Photography/Alamy Stock Photo; p. 9 (UConn logo) File:Connecticut Huskies wordmark.svg/Wikimedia Commons; p. 9 (UCLA logo) File:UCLA Bruins script.svg/Wikimedia Commons; p. 9 (main) TonyTheTiger/File:20170213 Villanova-Depaul Kris Jenkins in the backcourt.jpg/Wikimedia Commons; p. 10 File:Bill russell dribbling.jpg/Wikimedia Commons; p. 11 (main) Troutfarm27/File:Lakers banners & retired jerseys 2022.jpg/Wikimedia Commons; p. 11 (inset) TMP - An Instant of Time/Shutterstock.com; p. 13 Hasbi _Creative/Shutterstock.com; p. 15 UPI/Alamy Stock Photo; pp. 16, 22, 23 (left) Lorie Shaull/Flickr.com; p. 18 Vitalii Vitleo/Shutterstock.com; p. 19 (background) PhotOleh/Shutterstoc.com; p. 20 Michael Berlfein/Shutterstock.com; p. 21 (top) Zuma Press, Inc./Alamy Stock Photo; p. 21 (bottom) Michael Tipton/Flickr.com; p. 24 The White House/Flickr.com; p. 25 (background) Creativa Images/Shutterstock.com; p. 26 St.Rosenzweig/ File:Silbermedaille Olympische Spiele Münschen 1972.jpg/Wikimedia Commons; p. 27 (left) ilapinto/Shutterstock.com; p. 27 (right) Boris15/Shutterstock.com; p. 28 Master1305/Shutterstock.com; p. 29 (inset) File:Wes Unseld and Kareem Abdul-Jabbar.jpeg/Wikimedia Commons; p. 29 (main) courtesy of Library of Congress.

All rights reserved. No part of this book may be reproduced in any form without permission in writing from the publisher, except by a reviewer.

Printed in the United States of America

Some of the images in this book illustrate individuals who are models. The depictions do not imply actual situations or events.

CPSIA compliance information: Batch #CW25ENS: For further information contact Enslow Publishing, at 1-800-398-2504.

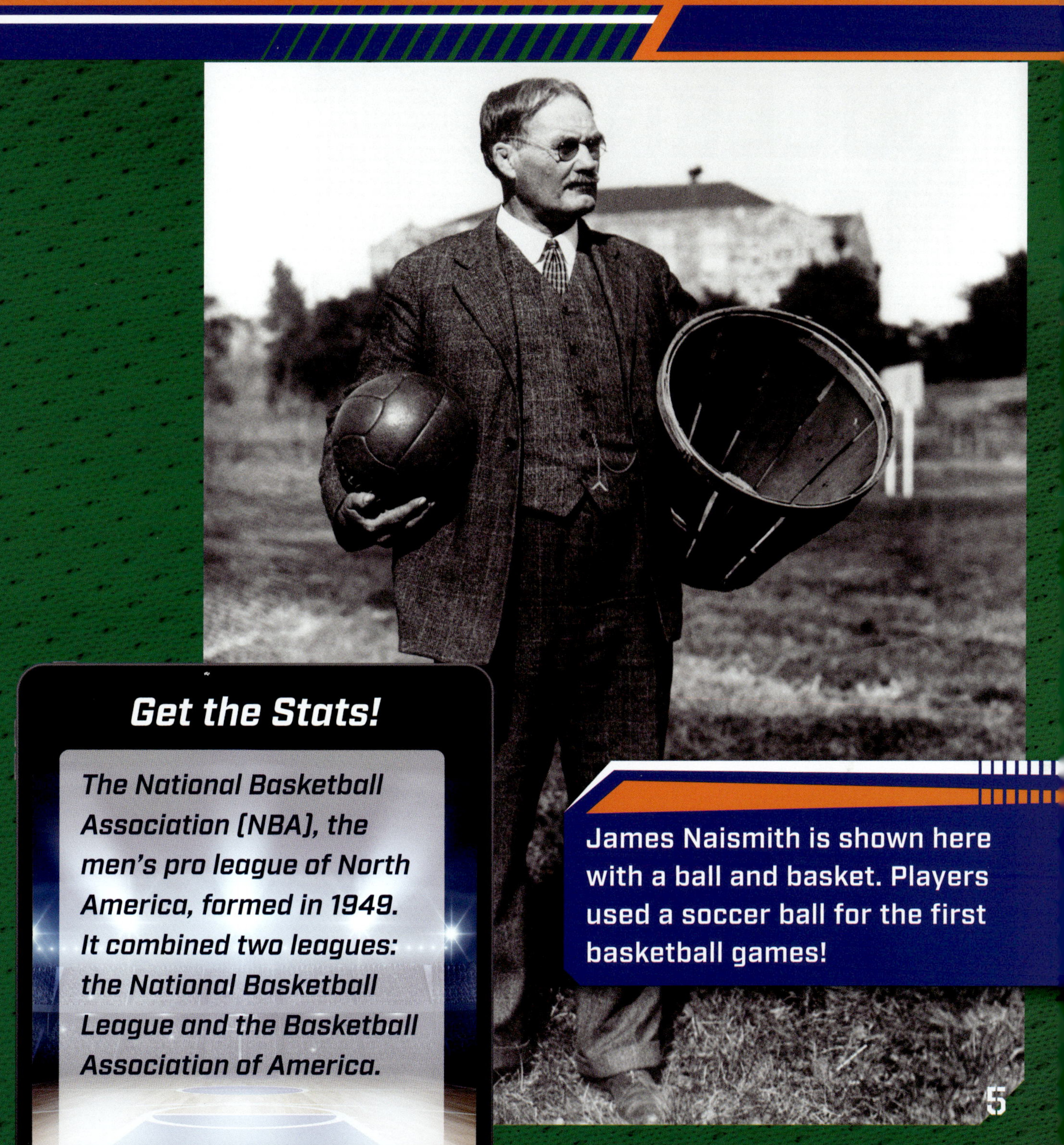

Get the Stats!

The National Basketball Association (NBA), the men's pro league of North America, formed in 1949. It combined two leagues: the National Basketball League and the Basketball Association of America.

James Naismith is shown here with a ball and basket. Players used a soccer ball for the first basketball games!

COLLEGE MADNESS

Most NBA and Women's National Basketball Association (WNBA) superstars played college basketball first. College players hold mind-blowing records, just like the pros.

The highest-scoring college player of all time is Caitlin Clark. She scored 3,951 points during her four years with the University of Iowa Hawkeyes. This number easily beat the record held by Louisiana State's Pete Maravich (3,667 points). Clark is also the first college player to record at least 3,800 points, 1,000 assists, and 950 rebounds.

PETE MARAVICH

CAITLIN CLARK

Clark became the top WNBA **draft** pick in 2024. The Indiana Fever chose her.

Get the Stats!

About 18.7 million people watched the 2024 National Collegiate Athletic Association (NCAA) **Championship** *between the University of Iowa and the University of South Carolina. That's the most for any women's basketball game. It was Clark's last game as a Hawkeye.*

LAST SHOTS

The NCAA **Division** 1 men's basketball **tournament** is called March Madness. In 1982, the Georgetown University Hoyas and University of North Carolina Tar Heels played for the Division 1 championship. With seconds left and the Tar Heels down by 1 point, a North Carolina freshman guard sank the game-winning shot. His name? Michael Jordan.

In 2016, the Tar Heels and Villanova Wildcats were tied in the championship game's second half. It looked like the teams were going to overtime when Wildcat Kris Jenkins sank a 3-pointer at the buzzer.

Kris Jenkins's 3-pointer is the only buzzer-beating shot to win a Division 1 men's basketball championship.

Get the Stats!

The University of California, Los Angeles (UCLA) Bruins have won the most NCAA Division I men's basketball championships with 11. The University of Connecticut Huskies have won the most NCAA Division I women's basketball championships with 11.

DYNASTIES

The NBA has seen some powerhouse teams since it began. Some became dynasties, or teams that keep winning season after season. That was the case for the Boston Celtics. During the years that center Bill Russell played for Boston, 1956 to 1969, the Celtics won a mind-blowing 11 championships in 13 seasons.

BILL RUSSELL

Get the Stats!

The Chicago Bulls won six championships between 1990 and 1998.

The Los Angeles Lakers under Magic Johnson was another dynasty. With Johnson as point guard from 1979 to 1991, the Lakers went to nine NBA Finals, winning five championships.

MAGIC JOHNSON STATUE

As of 2024, the Boston Celtics have the most NBA Championships with 18. After winning the 2024 Finals, they passed the Los Angeles Lakers, who have 17 championships. In third place are the Golden State Warriors with seven championship titles.

AIR JORDAN VS. KING JAMES

Two names often come up when people talk about the greatest basketball player ever: Michael Jordan and LeBron James. Jordan, nicknamed Air Jordan for his airtime while dunking, won six NBA championships with the Bulls. Jordan was the NBA's 10-time scoring champion and still leads the league in **career** average points per game.

James has won four NBA championships with three teams, the Miami Heat, the Cleveland Cavaliers, and the Lakers. In 2023, "King James" became the NBA all-time leading scorer. He passed 40,000 points in 2024.

Get the Stats!

After the 1987–1988 season, Michael Jordan was voted NBA MVP, ***Defensive*** *Player of the Year, and the scoring champion. No other player has achieved this.*

STACKING THE STATS: JORDAN VS. LEBRON (SO FAR)

(as of August 2024)

Michael Jordan	statistic	Lebron James
15	number of years in the NBA	21
6	number of championships won	4
1,072	NBA games played	1,492
24,537	field goals attempted	29,313
12,192	field goals made	14,837
30.1	career average points per game	27.1
10	number of seasons with highest points in league	1
69	highest number of points in a game	61
581	career 3-pointers	2,410
32,292	career points	40,474
5	number of NBA MVP awards	4

Jordan retired in 2003, and James is still playing as of 2024. James will likely break new records, but some of Jordan's NBA **statistics** seem unbeatable.

CURRY WITH THE 3!

In basketball, forwards such as LeBron James and Michael Jordan often get the glory, but every position is key to winning. Point guard Stephen "Steph" Curry is perhaps the brightest star for the Golden State Warriors. In 2016, he scored a record no one else has: he was the only player in NBA history to be voted MVP **unanimously**.

A shorter player at 6 feet (1.83 m) tall, Curry is known for his great ball-handling and his long 3-point shot. In 2016, he sunk the most 3-pointers ever in a season (402). In 2021, he became the all-time 3-point leader.

Get the Stats!

In 2015–2016, the Warriors had the best regular-season record in NBA history, 73–9.

As of 2024, the Warriors have won the NBA Championship four times with Steph Curry (2015, 2017, 2018, and 2022).

SUPER ASSISTERS

Not all statistics, or stats, in basketball are about points. A great player knows when not to take the shot and when to pass it to the teammate who has the best chance of sinking it. The all-time NBA assist leader is Utah Jazz point guard John Stockton. Between 1984 and 2003, he made 15,806 assists. It's a record that likely won't be broken.

Get the Stats!

The all-time leader for steals in the WNBA is Tamika Catchings with 1,074. Sue Bird holds the record for assists with 3,234. Both records are several hundred ahead of second place.

SUE BIRD

Stockton had a 19-year career with the Jazz, during which the team never missed the playoffs.

Stockton could make plays happen for the Jazz. He also has the most steals of any player, an incredible 3,265.

DEFENSE!

Defensive players don't get the glory, but you want them on your team! Blocks and rebounds are stats that reflect good defensive skills. Wilt Chamberlain, who played from 1959 to 1973, is the all-time leader in rebounds with an amazing 23,924 and the single-game record with 55.

Get the Stats!

In 2024, Rudy Gobert, a center for the Minnesota Timberwolves, was named Defensive Player of the Year for the fourth time, tying the record.

Chamberlain also holds the record for most points in a game, with 100 points, scored in a 1962 game between the Philadelphia Warriors and the New York Knicks.

Hakeem Olajuwon, who played from 1984 to 2002, owns the record for most blocks with 3,830. Lakers center Elmore Smith posted the most blocks in a single game with 17, a record he's held since 1973.

DRAFT-DAY GAMBLE

When a team picks a player in the draft, they're guessing—and hoping—the player will help them win. At the 1987 NBA Draft, the San Antonio Spurs took a chance with their number-one pick. They chose center David Robinson. Why was this a risk?

Robinson had attended the U.S. Naval Academy and had to serve a number of years in the U.S. Navy after school. The Spurs waited two more years for Robinson, but the risk paid off. During his pro career, Robinson won NBA **Rookie** of the Year, NBA MVP, and Defensive Player of the Year.

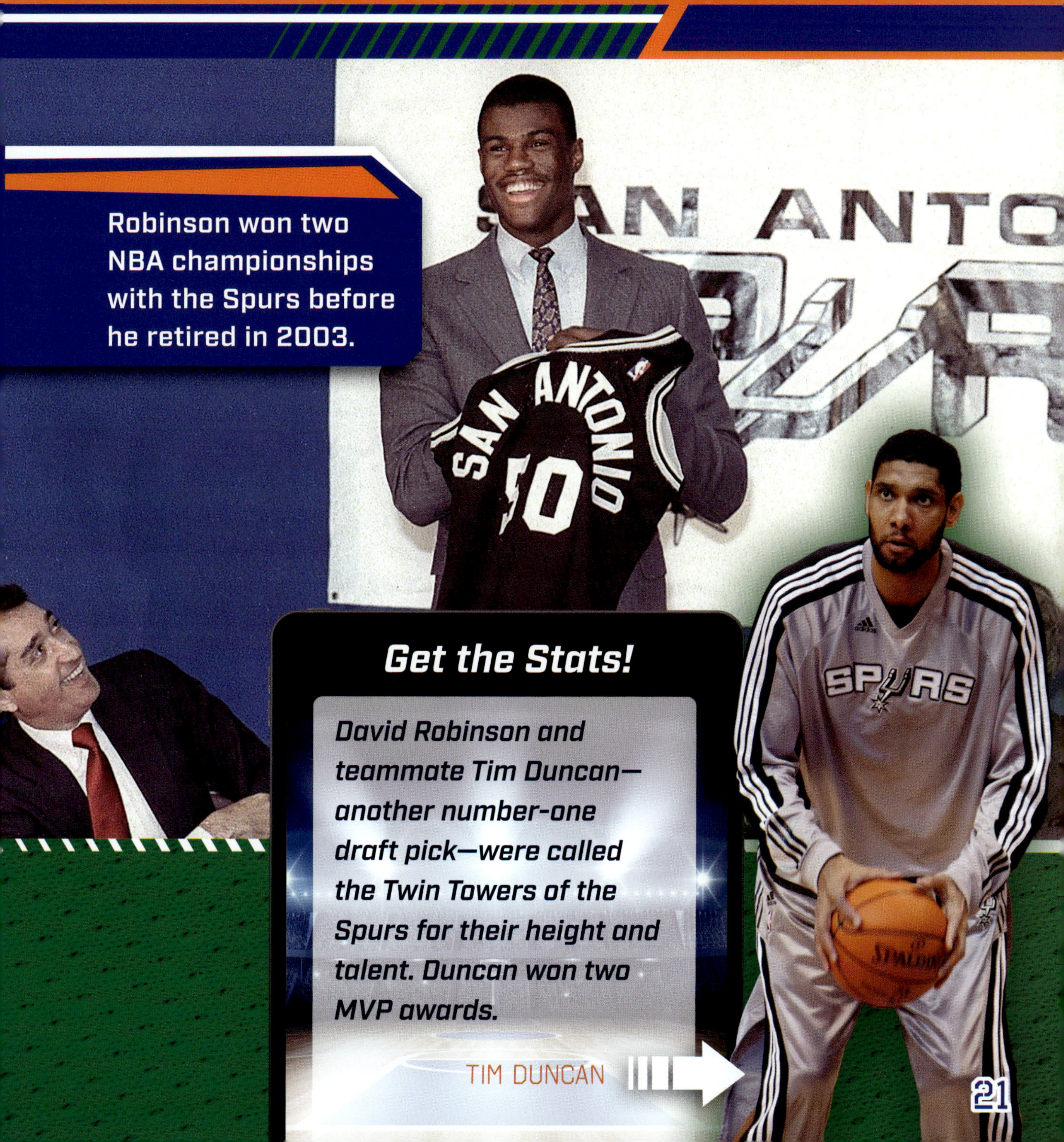

Robinson won two NBA championships with the Spurs before he retired in 2003.

Get the Stats!

David Robinson and teammate Tim Duncan—another number-one draft pick—were called the Twin Towers of the Spurs for their height and talent. Duncan won two MVP awards.

TIM DUNCAN

THE WNBA WOWS

The WNBA began in 1997 with eight teams and became the most successful U.S. women's pro sports league ever. Early superstars include Sheryl Swoopes, Rebecca Lobo, Lisa Leslie, and Cynthia Cooper, who are all now in the Naismith Basketball Hall of Fame.

In 2024, the 12-team WNBA reported its highest attendance ever in the first month of play. Fans were excited by the high level of play that rookies, such as Caitlin Clark and Angel Reese, brought to the court.

In June 2024, Angel Reese set a new single-season WNBA record, posting 10 double-doubles in a row. A double-double is when a player has double figures, or 10 or more, in two of the five main stats in basketball: points, assists, rebounds, blocks, and steals.

DIANA TAURASI

Get the Stats!

As of August 2024, three-time WNBA champion Diana Taurasi is the league's all-time leading scorer, with more than 10,000 points.

OLYMPIC EXCELLENCE

As of 2024, the U.S. men's basketball team has won a medal in all 20 **Olympics** it has entered, winning gold 17 times. The 1992 Olympics was the first that allowed pro players. The U.S. team was nicknamed the Dream Team for its unmatched talent.

The 1996 U.S. women's Olympic team had a big task—they had to be good enough to win gold and get crowds excited for the launch, or start, of the WNBA. The players, including Dawn Staley and Sheryl Swoopes, went 8–0 on their way to the gold. Future WNBA stars remember being **inspired** by this team.

DAWN STALEY AND VICE PRESIDENT KAMALA HARRIS, 2024

THE 1992 MEN'S OLYMPIC BASKETBALL TEAM

PLAYER	POSITION	TEAM
Charles Barkley	forward	Phoenix Suns
Chris Mullin	forward/guard	Golden State Warriors
Christian Laettner	forward/center	Duke University
Clyde Drexler	guard	Portland Trail Blazers
David Robinson	center	San Antonio Spurs
John Stockton	point guard	Utah Jazz
Karl Malone	forward	Utah Jazz
Larry Bird	forward	Boston Celtics
Magic Johnson	point guard	Los Angeles Lakers (retired 1991)
Michael Jordan	forward	Chicago Bulls
Patrick Ewing	center	New York Knicks
Scottie Pippen	forward	Chicago Bulls

Famous **rivals** Magic Johnson and Larry Bird were co-captains of the unbeaten 1992 gold medal team.

VICTORY AND DEFEAT

The 1972 U.S. men's Olympic basketball team had another first: the first Olympic team in any sport to refuse medals! In the final, Team USA was winning against the Soviet Union by 1 point with 1 second left when a Soviet coach claimed they had called time out with 3 seconds left.

Play began with 2 more seconds. The Soviets passed in the ball and didn't score. But the official clock hadn't been reset. Play began again with 3 seconds left, and the Soviets scored. Team USA believed these events were unfair.

The 1972 U.S. men's national basketball team was the youngest in its history.

Get the Stats!

The record holder for scoring in Olympic basketball has never won a medal! Brazilian Oscar Schmidt played in five Olympics. He has the records for most points (1,093) and most points in a game (55).

THE FUTURE OF BASKETBALL

Future basketball stars of the NBA, WNBA, and Olympics are playing now. They may be sinking 3s in their driveway and blocking shots at the park. Many of the all-time greats, including Kareem Abdul-Jabbar and Kobe Bryant, perfected their skills in high school. Abdul-Jabbar's high school team won 71 games in a row, and Bryant was so good he went right to the NBA!

Who will be the next great star? Keep practicing, and it might be you!

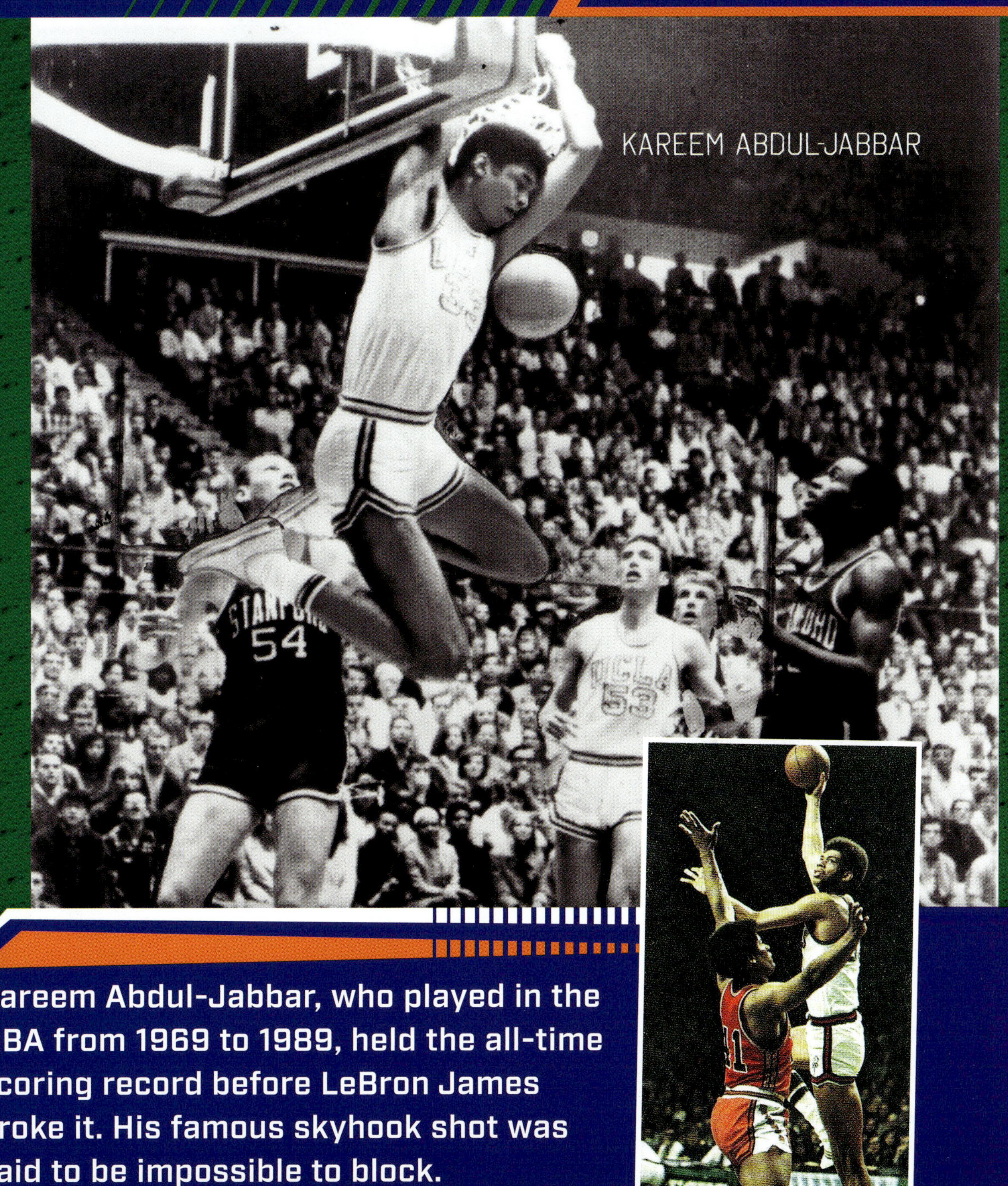

Kareem Abdul-Jabbar, who played in the NBA from 1969 to 1989, held the all-time scoring record before LeBron James broke it. His famous skyhook shot was said to be impossible to block.

GLOSSARY

career: The whole amount of time someone spends at a job.

championship: Events that decide the overall winner of a sport or contest.

defensive: Guarding against opponents, or the team you're playing against.

division: A group of teams or people who compete against each other.

draft: The process of selecting players from a pool of potential players entering a sports league.

engage: To hold the interest of.

inspire: To cause someone to want to do something.

Olympics: Also called the Olympic Games, an international sports competition held once every two years, switching back and forth between summer and winter games.

rival: A person or group who tries to be more successful than another.

rookie: A player during their first year in the league.

statistics: Information that can be related in numbers. "Stats" is the shortened form.

tournament: A series of contests testing the skill of many athletes in the same sport.

unanimously: Agreed on by everyone.

FOR MORE INFORMATION

BOOKS

Berglund, Bruce. *Basketball GOATs: The Greatest Athletes of All Time.* North Mankato, MN: Capstone Press, 2022.

Buckley, James. *Big Book of Who: Basketball.* Chicago, IL: Triumph Books LLC, 2022.

Flynn, Brendan. Sue *Bird vs. Candace Parker: Basketball Legends Face Off.* North Mankato, MN: Capstone Press, 2025.

WEBSITES

Basketball Reference
www.basketball-reference.com/
This is a source for the stats of the top basketball leagues.

National Geographic Kids: Bonkers About Basketball
www.natgeokids.com/uk/kids-club/entertainment/general-entertainment/bonkers-about-basketball/
Learn about the pros as well as the NBA league for young people.

Science Kids: Fun Basketball Facts for Kids
www.sciencekids.co.nz/sciencefacts/sports/basketball.html
Check out some facts that will surprise you about this sport.

Publisher's note to educators and parents: Our editors have carefully reviewed these websites to ensure that they are suitable for students. Many websites change frequently, however, and we cannot guarantee that a site's future contents will continue to meet our high standards of quality and educational value. Be advised that students should be closely supervised whenever they access the internet.

INDEX